NORMAN ROCKWELL'S
AMERICAN FISHERMAN

Written by Milton Garrison

CRESCENT BOOKS
New York

Illustrations reprinted under license from
the Estate of Norman Rockwell.

Copyright © 1990 Estate of Norman Rockwell

Photographic material courtesy of
The Norman Rockwell Museum at
Stockbridge, Stockbridge, MA

Created and manufactured by arrangement with
Ottenheimer Publishers, Inc.

Copyright © 1990 Ottenheimer Publishers, Inc.
This 1990 edition is published by Ottenheimer
Publishers, Inc. for Crescent Books,
distributed by Crown Publishers, Inc.,
225 Park Avenue South, New York, New York 10003

Printed and bound in Hong Kong.

ISBN: 0-517-67899-3
h g f e d c b

Contents

INTRODUCTION   9

CHAPTER I   13
Fishing

CHAPTER II   25
Fishing People

CHAPTER III   33
How They Catch Fish

CHAPTER IV   61
Tackle and Gear

CHAPTER V   73
Baits and Lures

CHAPTER VI   85
The Fish

SPRING ● WINTER

norman rockwell

Spring-Winter (1934)

INTRODUCTION

Fishing is an integral part of the American experience Norman Rockwell painted during six decades. It remains a touchstone and a tradition in this country, as American as baseball, the Fourth of July, and the Thanksgiving turkey dinner.

It was estimated that there were more than 40 million fisherman at the time of Norman Rockwell's death, in 1978. That number continues to grow, and it is a remarkable one. In recent years, enthusiasts have supported a modest number of television programs devoted to the sport and, on occasion, lined the shores of lakes to observe and encourage favorites in fishing contests. The definition of a fisherman is more stringent than that of a baseball, basketball, or football fan. It includes active participants only. A fisherman goes fishing.

The works of Norman Rockwell delved into the continuing American love affair with fishing. It is not a distinctly American pursuit, of course. Millennia ago, prehistoric man went to the ocean shores, to lakes and streams in his all-important search for food. He fashioned primitive bone fish-hooks and spears as early as he took up hunting. As long as 2,000 years ago, man was tying flies to entice fresh-water fish to snap up an artificial insect. Archaeologists and anglers call that earliest known lure the Macedonian.

Norman Rockwell's paintings reflect this interest in fishing. The boy who set off with a cane pole, a cotton line, and live bait usually lived close to the fishing hole. The chores he was evading probably were cutting wood and carrying it to keep the house warm in winter as well as for the kitchen range, watering and feeding the stock, and helping with the milking twice a day.

Norman Rockwell's work reflects much of that earlier America, and in particular the opportunities for adventure it held for the young. His first sales of work were to outdoor and adventure publications directed to young boys. These were many pen-and-ink drawings on how-to-do-it in the outdoors: camping, packing, cooking, care of the feet, even how to load and pack a horse. Illustrations also included drawings of the flies and larvae that attract fish.

From 1913 onwards, he regularly published covers and illustrated adventure tales. As his fame grew, his work appeared in general-interest publications, an old humor magazine, and many others, but he often returned to outdoor adventure themes. Fishing tales, fishing lore, and best of all, Norman Rockwell's inestimable artwork, lead us through this chronicle on fishing.

Man Killer (1940) 11

Across the Threshold (1914)

12

Chapter 1
Fishing

Fishing in Early America

Fishing for pastime as well as for food had been established from time immemorial in the Old World by the time the first Europeans settled in the New. They brought with them their hobby and their fishing gear and techniques. It could not have surprised them that the original inhabitants also fished, although they were duly impressed with the American Indian practice of using fish leftovers to fertilize cornhills. We can imagine their delight, though, at the fishing. Here were clear pristine streams, hardly fished at all in comparison to the tired waters back home. The fish stories must have been heroic.

The fishing continued good on the American continent for centuries. Lewis and Clark, mapping the Northwest for President Thomas Jefferson at the turn of the Eighteenth Century, found more and more virgin rivers and streams, and reported new species of game- and food-fish frequently. A hundred years later, the population had only begun to consolidate the expansion westward. Throughout the country, streams—some yet to be discovered—ran pure. The fish abounded, fat and sassy.

In the Land of Gold (1915)

America was a distinctive country by then, with a character all its own. This was the land that Mark Twain and Bret Harte wrote of. If things didn't work out on the home farm or the hardware store, the frontier was there for the stout-hearted. With a grubstake and a loaded mule, many struck out on their own for adventure and wealth. All things were possible in America. The outlook was optimistic, free-wheeling, big as all outdoors. Even the lies were on a grandiose scale. And there was a lot of outdoors. Americans were building their railroads, taking up homesteads, enjoying their elbow-room, looking to the frontier.

This was the America that Norman Rockwell was born into, and the country that he painted faithfully from 1912, when he was 18. Perhaps the great appeal of his depictions of the fishing experience is that to the modern American—fisherman or not—the paintings are a connection to that earlier, untroubled, and exuberant nation. In our American consciousness and folk memory, the grass was greener, the air more bracing, the life more simple. And there was plenty of room. It is a country in which just about any kid could, like Tom Sawyer or Huckleberry Finn, dig up a can-full of earthworms, stroll along bosky paths to the riverbank, bait a hook, throw in the line, and forget the restrictions of chores and civilization as he lay on the bank and waited for the fish to bite.

Tell-Me-Why Stories (1912) 15

Growing Up with Fishing

Johnny released the last armload of stovewood from a high position, so that it would thump and clatter. Mother and the girls would know he was hard at work on his chores. Through the screen-door and open windows he heard the regular thump from the front porch where Mother was churning, and smelled the sharp aroma of sweet milk turning to butter. The buttermilk, after chilling a few hours in the spring house, would go well with the mess of fish he planned to bring home.

He heard the murmurs as his sisters Annie and Catherine chatted companionably with Mother, rocking in the old high-backed rocking chairs and stringing and snapping the beans he'd picked earlier in the kitchen garden. In the pauses in conversation, over the thump of the dasher on the bottom of the churn, came the ping of the beans as they struck the tin boiler. It was pleasant on the porch, shaded from the sun's heat and catching the occasional light breeze. He thought he might take a chair there, snap a few beans and talk. But it was not to take part in a ladies' social that he had begged off joining Father and George in the hayfield. He had other fish to fry.

He brushed the splinters and bits of bark off the front of his bib-overalls. Thirsty work, chopping wood. He lifted the cheesecloth and dipped himself a drink from the enameled pail on the kitchen table, held the dipper at the end of its long handle, and drank slowly. He'd carried the water down from the spring that morning, and it was still cold. He tossed the water through the screen-door and into the yard with a practiced twist of his wrist and replaced the dipper next to the pail.

Johnny opened the food-safe and took from a covered dish the piece of pork rind he'd talked mother out of the day before. He might just go after Old Unreconstructed, the catfish that hung around the channel under that leaning elm. He put the pork rind in his right-hand pocket, with a cork, his spare string, kitchen matches, lead weights, best shooting marble, jackknife, and other necessities. He spotted a plateful of biscuits left over from breakfast and stuck one, then another, in his left pocket, the clean one.

He closed the perforated metal door of the food-safe and fastened it. Then he went through the dining-room and parlor to the entry hall, and picked out one of the tall cane fishing poles, leaning in the corner behind the coat-tree. He was ready to go fishing.

As he closed the screen door, holding it against the spring to avoid slamming it, Mother sang out, "Bring me a nice mess of fish, Johnny."

Boy and Dog (1941) 17

Bill, napping in the shade of the plum tree, yawned, stretched fore and aft, and scampered to join him, tail wagging hard. They ambled up the path to the woodshed. After digging up the worms in the barnyard before milking time, he'd placed them deep in the shade there. They were still lively, writhing in and out of dirt he'd put in the can with them.

Johnny's bare toes luxuriated in the fine warm dust of the wagon tracks as they walked to the gate. Thinking about school again in a month or so, he knew then he'd have to wear shoes again. Bill went off on various excursions in the fields and woods as he scented rabbits and chipmunks, but always returned, tongue lolling. On the road, they met Mr. Appleyard and the boys, hauling a load of shelled corn with their team of gray mules, to Meeks's mill for grinding. They exchanged greetings. "Good day for fishing," Mr. Appleyard said. "You may have to hide behind a tree to bait your hook."

Bill, off again, was waiting for him at the turn-off to the creek. Now the forest took over on either side of the path. The shade deepened and the bird songs were varied. In a quarter-mile, they were at his fishing spot. Johnny cut a forked sapling with his jackknife, sharpened the end, and stuck it in the ground. He freed the fishhook and unfurled the line from the pole. He considered and decided on a bass or maybe a sunfish. He'd try Old Unreconstructed later.

He tied a cork on the line, scrabbled in the bait-can for a fat, appetising worm, and fixed it on the hook. Then he tossed the line in, propped the base of the pole in the fork of the sapling, held it down with one foot, and sat down with his back against an oak. He watched the cork and thought about things.

The boy who baited his hook with worms or doughballs to catch a satisfying mess of panfish was likely in later life to seek out more adventurous fish in more remote waters, and to do so in the company of friends, or with his wife or children. That amounts to a fishing expedition, and the expedition is a transforming experience in itself. At its best, it is a renewal of the contact with nature.

The Haunted Hollow (1914)

The Fishing Expedition

"I've got some mighty nice trout today," the dining-car waiter said.

"No thank you," said John. "We'll be eating rainbows we caught ourselves this evening. I'll have the Maryland fried chicken."

"This guy's an optimist," Cliff told the waiter with a smile. "But I'll have the chicken too. Never know your luck."

They finished lunch as the train arrived, and as it chugged away they were changing in the depot washroom from their citified traveling clothes. They emerged with their suits and ties rolled in the packs on their backs, ready to hike and to fish, in lumberjack shirts, canvas vests with plenty of pockets for trout-flies and gear, and waterproof canvas trousers tucked into thick, laced boots. Both wore floppy hats, with trout flies arranged in the bands.

"You know the way, Cliff," said John, and followed as his friend strode down the main street of the small town. They headed toward the road, lane, and path that led to the trout stream.

They spoke little on the path in the heavy woods, falling into the rhythm and swing of men on the trail, savoring the crisp air, the hum of insects, and the calls of jays and, farther off, a loon. John heard the stream rush and gurgle before they got to the clearing on its bank. They shrugged out of the packstraps, eased their loads to the ground, and walked to the water's edge.

"I think you picked a good one," said John. "Oh, there's trout in this stream, all right, and smallmouth bass and what-not," said Cliff. "We used to come here every spring or summer before the War, Dad and

20

Mom and all us kids. We'd carry in potatoes and bake 'em in the camp-fire, and cans of pork and beans. Went good with the fish, if we caught fish. When we didn't, we ate beans and baked potatoes."

John laughed easily. "I brought some bacon and some canned pork and beans, just in case," he said. "But I still think we'll get fish to go with them. Let's set up camp and get back here and catch ourselves some dinner, eh?"

The two friends took the horseshoe rolls off their packs and removed the Army blankets rolled in the shelter-halves. Then they found an elevated, smooth patch of ground and set up the pup-tent, just as they had often done in more pressing situations in France. John used the flat of a hand-axe and Cliff the back of a small spade to hammer in the pegs that tightened and anchored the sides. John gathered pine needles to cushion the ground under the canvas, then carefully spread a blanket over them.

"Good thing we both brought spare blankets," Cliff said. "It gets cold back here this time of year when the sun goes down."

"I'm hungry, too," said John. "You bring the skillet?"

"Yep, and the coffee and the coffee-pot, too. You bring some bread?"

The buddies unloaded their packs, stowed their gear and utensils, and carefully leaned their two-piece fly-rods, still in their flannel cases, against out-of-the-way trees. In a few minutes, camp was ready. Cliff gathered dry brush and fallen limbs for firewood, and John lopped it into handy size with the little axe. Together, they built a field-stove of large rocks, placing a metal grille over it to support pots and pans.

"Tell you what," Cliff offered. "I'll set us up and get some coffee going. You go on and try your luck with the rainbows before it gets dark."

John carried his rod-case and fly-box to the bank. He removed the rod sections from the case, and rubbed the ferrule tip against his nose to lubricate it. Then he carefully lined up the line guides before gently sliding the ferrule home. With the reel mounted, the line threaded through the guides, and the leader tied on, he considered the fly or bait he would use.

He gazed at the rushing stream and into the clear water. In the morning sun he'd be able to see the fish feeding below the surface. From the woods, he heard a bob-white call. He heard a splash and spotted the flash of a fish. But there was no hatch going on, no insects swarming on the surface. He'd try a wet-fly, a nymph. If that didn't work, he wasn't too proud to use a worm.

He tied on a mayfly nymph and raised his rod to cast. It was quiet in the woods, and he smelled coffee now. He heard the plop of a fish. It was peaceful here.

That communion with nature is the link with the American past we find in Norman Rockwell's work. For the fisherman of today it is still out there. We may have to travel further, make a more sudden transition. We may even stay in a nearby "rustic" motel and dine on its menu instead of beans and bacon, and share the wilderness with more people than we really want to. But in memory, the expedition is suffused with the smell of woodsmoke, the slowly rising mist, the sounds of insects, frogs, night-creatures, jumping fish and the quiet contemplation of nature. Little wonder that the boy whose Mom discovered his mumps just on the brink of a fishing trip was so disappointed.

Mumps (1972)

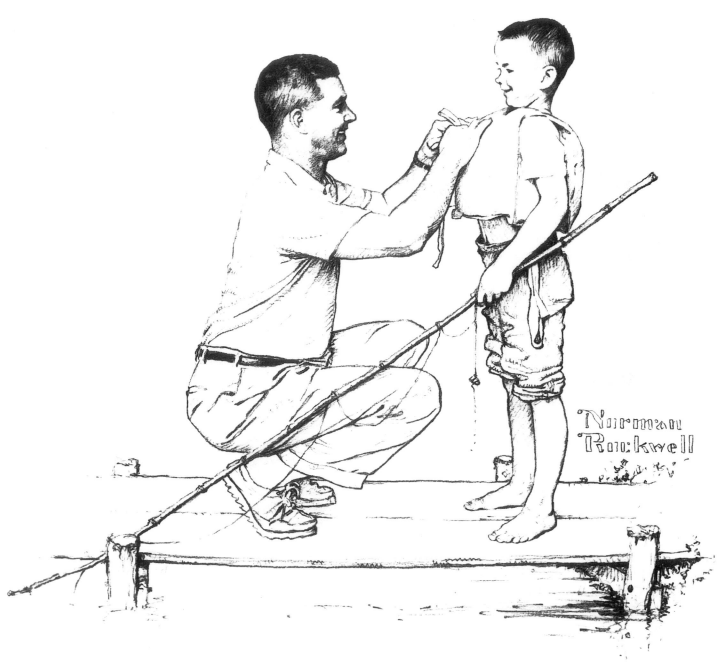

Boy and Dad on Dock (1960)

Chapter 2
Fishing People

Rites of Passage

Fishing embraces all sorts and conditions of men and women. Most often the love of fishing is passed down through the generations, from parents to sons and daughters. Often, it is a lifelong pursuit.

Usually (and using the masculine, as we shall throughout, to include both genders), a boy's first experience of fishing is one of the rites of passage, a milestone in the transition from protected childhood to independent adult pursuits. In most cases, it is the father who makes the introduction, on a family outing to a nearby stream or pond, or an ocean pier. The father may be a sophisticated angler for trout or salmon, or a great catcher of the deep-sea prizes, but for this initiation he uses the simple tools and methods his father first taught him in pursuit of simple fish.

"But you said you'd teach me to fish, Daddy."

"And I will, Chuckie. But Mummy likes to fish, too, and she's got to take care of Sister now. We'll all go after lunch, O.K.?"

"Aw, Daddy."

"Oh, take him now, John," says Kathleen. "You'll just be hanging around in the way here, and you know I don't like the way you cook hamburgers. I'll call you when lunch is ready, and we can all go down with the baby afterwards, when she takes her nap."

"All right, Kathy. Pick up your fishing pole, son, and let's get going."

John carries Charlie's lightest rod over his shoulder, pulling his hand to speed him up, as they walk from the picnic table to the pond.

"Will we eat it if I catch one, Daddy?"

"Sure, son. Long as he's big enough."

On the bank, John knots the transparent leader to the line. Charlie watches, goggle-eyed.

"What's that for, Daddy?"

"So the fish won't see the line, son. We want him to think the minnow's all by himself. He might get frightened if he saw the line."

John fishes a minnow out of a cardboard carton and impales it on the hook. The boy's eyes widen again. He is excited, but a little queasy now. John shows him the knots, and explains why they won't slip. He also explains the brightly painted float and the weight he pinches around the line with a small pair of pliers.

"The weight keeps the minnow down where we want it, see, and the float keeps it from going down to the bottom. Sunfishes mostly swim near the surface, not on the bottom."

He finishes the preparations and pats the boy's slender back. "All right now, son. You're ready to fish."

He hands the rod to Charlie and keeps an unobtrusive grip on it as he coaches the boy in tossing the minnow into the water.

"I'm fishing," Charlie chortles.

"You certainly are," says John.

26

And nothing happens.

"Why?" Charlie asks. "When do I catch my fish?"

"You've got to wait for the fish," John answers. "They'll bite when they're ready. Ask Mom. But you've got to be patient."

"But how will I know when he bites? What do they do?"

"You'll know, all right," says John. "Hold that rod loose—not too loosely, now. You'll feel it when he bites."

"What's it feel like?"

"Depends on the size. He may nibble around at first. You'll feel that. But don't do anything yet. When he grabs it hard and runs with it, you'll really know it. Watch that cork, too. When he pulls that down, then you jerk up that pole up and hook him good."

Father and son sit side by side in the quiet, and watch the cork and the ripples on the water.

"How big do you think he'll be, Dad? Can we eat him? Do you think the minnow's still on the hook? Do you think he's still alive? Shall I bring the line back so we can see?"

"Shhh, son. The fish don't like noise. They won't bite when you're talking."

Eventually, the cork jiggles slightly. The boy feels a vibration in the pole, transmitted along the line from the nuzzling fish. He tenses, and looks apprehensively at John.

John senses the impending strike, too. "Wait, now," he says, quietly. "Wait till he takes it."

The boy feels a flutter. The cork goes under. Now there's an electrifying surge pulling at the line. He pulls the pole up abruptly, not noticing John's hand on the rod again to add authority to the yank.

"You've hooked him, son. Bring him in," says John.

The Best Fishing

As the initiate grows older, he may stick to fishing for the panfish-sunfish or bream in the local stream, or the catfish in a nearby river channel. These give good sport and they are delicious, especially fresh-caught. Or he may go further afield for trout or salmon, universally recognized as the aristocrats of gamefish in America. Panfish are the first love, and a lifelong one, for many a fisherman. The reasons for this continuing affection are evident. The various sunfishes, together with the white perch and yellow perch, are lumped together as panfish. All are tasty, relatively easy to catch, and fun. The sunfish is the most familiar to American fishermen, and the most sought by boys with fishing poles and cans of worms in our folk-memory and in Norman Rockwell's paintings. It is native only to North America, and it swims a great number of the streams rivers, ponds and lakes of the continent from southern Canada to Northern Mexico, in every state but Alaska. Moreover, light gear permits these undiscriminating little fish to give the fisherman a fight, if only a minor one.

Fish in the sea, particularly gamefish, run larger than those in fresh water. For that reason, fishermen use heavier and stronger rods, reels, lines, leaders, and lures for them. The fisherman trusts the fish to provide all the tension needed for a challenging battle. A great many fishermen go to great lengths for savage, hard-fighting bass of all varieties. Many thousands of people spend much of their winters fishing through the ice of frozen lakes for a variety of fish. Others take to the deep seas, for big-game excitement and spectacular trophies.

Fishermen of all persuasions go after trout with minnows, worms, and other live bait, as well as with artificial flies, spinners, spoons, and plugs. In lakes, the best fishing is in early morning and twilight, when the fish rise to feed near the surface. At other times, trout favor deep holes. In streams and rivers, the brook trout collect to feed at eddies or backwaters created by brush, underwater rocks, or fallen trees. That's where flies, bait, or lures get results.

The Scout Merit Badge of Angling (1914)

Many fishermen dabble in whatever fishing is at hand. He will use the bait, lures, and tackle for the local fish. To learn what those are, all he needs to do is ask a local fisherman or inquire at a tackle-and-bait shop. Fishing is a non-exclusive fraternity that has members from all professions and trades, all financial conditions including those who literally fish for food. They have in common that communion with nature as well as the excitement of the electrifying strike on the line and the battle that follows.

Charlie leads Annie down to the dock for her first afternoon of fishing. John was going to supervise this expedition, but he's back in the cabin, dealing on the telephone with a snag that's come up in the office. Kathleen also wanted to come, but the new baby has colic, and she is soothing her in a quiet bedroom.

The boy baits Annie's hook for her, and points out a school of sunfish feeding in the shallows around the supports for the pier.

"They're pretty," Annie says.

"Drop the worm down there, Annie, right in amongst 'em."

The sunnies slow their swimming. One of them investigates the worm, nibbles at it.

"Not yet," Charlie whispers. "Wait 'til he grabs it."

The sunfish, satisfied with his nibble, grabs the worm and the hook.

"Now, hook him. Jerk that rod up," Charlie shouts. The little girl does, and quickly Charlie is working the hook out of the flopping little fish's mouth.

"Let's get another one," Annie says.

"We can come back later. Let's get in the boat and try those lily pads over there."

Annie sits in the prow as Charlie rows the boat to a spot where he's caught larger fish, pumpkinseeds and even smallmouth bass, feeding among the weeds. Now he cautions Annie to be patient and quiet, as they dabble light bait near the surface. Soon, though, patience is rewarded with a strike. And the pumpkinseed is made of sterner stuff than the smaller fish near the shore. There's no nibble, just an explosion of jumping and thrashing, as he pounces on the bait and runs with it.

A Double Gift (1915)

Now there's a flopping little fish in the boat. Farther out, mooching around in deeper water near a submerged rock, there are good-sized crappies that will put a bend in the rod, carrying out line against the clicking drag mechanism of the reel.

They row back to the pier. "That's fun," Annie says. She spies Mom on the porch, rocking the baby.

"We caught some fish, Mom," she calls.

"Next time," Charlie promises her, "I'll row and we'll troll for bass. That's *really* a fish."

Fishing Grandfather and Boy (1954)

Chapter 3
How They Catch Fish

Nice and Easy

The simplest and easiest fishing is for the panfish with natural bait. It is the type of fishing on which most beginners learn. Often, the earliest fishing is done with Dad relaxing alongside an eager beginner where the fish are likely to be. He teaches the youngster how to handle a hand-line, where the fish he's looking for is likely to be, the depth at which it feeds, and the bait most likely to succeed. As Bill and Kathy learn more about fish and fishing, Dad graduates them to a rod and reel. A light, flexible rod allows the fisherman to feel the runs and maneuvers of the fish when it is hooked. The reel permits the eager angler to play the fish, giving it line to run with, and reeling in the line to keep it fairly taut. Dad shows why this is needed to avoid slack that would allow the fish to slip off the hook, or the line to snarl or catch on snags, rocks, or other obstructions. He demonstrates raising the rod to slow the fish's run and lowering it to horizontal; he gives the fish line.

Dad and his excited companion practice these basic techniques to fish a pond or a larger body of water for a number of different panfish. A school of sunfish feeding in the shallows may be sighted. The new fisherman lowers a worm on a hook into the school and waits for the sunnies to investigate and bite, prepared to impale another worm on a hook quickly, as soon as the brief struggle is over, and dangle it for another catch.

Unlike the larger and sportier varieties, most small panfish will nibble at the bait before deciding to gobble it up. When this happens, the tense fisherman must ignore the nibbles and wait for the grab. Then, and only then, he pulls up the end of the rod sharply, to seat the hook.

A Hushpuppy Story

"I love hushpuppies," said Jenny as she reached for another of the cornmeal dodgers, "Why do you suppose they named them that? Doesn't sound all that appetizing, does it?"

Charlie, very much in love with this girl, smiled fondly at her as he put down his fork.

"My father told me how hushpuppies got their name. That was long before people ever heard of catfish or hushpuppies, according to Dad."

Picnic on a Rocky Coast (1918)

"Catfish? I know that's what you're eating, but what's it got to do with hushpuppies?"

"Well, the way Dad tells it, it's all pretty country, and southern country, at that. I hear it was the same in the Midwest, but I know the way people in the South fished when my Dad was a kid, and the way they cooked almost any kind of fish, but especially a catfish.

"Whole families and clans would go fishing together in those days. Fewer distractions, you know. No television, not many radios and, in Dad's part of the country, no electricity to run one on. So they went on outings. They'd spend the day and maybe the night at it. They'd bring along the pots and pans and cooking stuff, build a fire, sit around and sing and tell stories, and they'd fish, come back to the fire, and fish some more. They'd catch sunfishes and bass—mostly largemouth down South."

"And catfish, of course," Jenny said.

"As you say. And then they'd cook 'em all up. That's where the Southern part comes in. In those days, they fried everything. And the way they liked to eat fish was with cornpone."

"Cornpone? You mean it really exists? What is it?"

"It's the same as cornbread, only it's thinner. You pour it into a skillet, fry it and flip it, and you've got a pone. You take a stack of pones and butter it and pour syrup or molasses on it, and you eat fried fish with it.

"Anyhow, with the whole family there, the dogs just naturally came along too, and when they smelled all that fish frying—"

"And all that grease."

"And all that grease, yes. With all those lovely smells, the dogs would start yapping and complaining for something to eat. Well, in those days a country dog didn't get much meat; he'd hunt for that. But I remember Grandma would always toss old Bill III and IV and all the other Bills a slab of cornbread after dinner, which was in the middle of the day. So out on the river bank, they'd fry up blobs of cornmeal batter and toss them to the dogs. They'd say hush, puppy."

Jenny regarded him with suspicion. "I don't believe that."

Charlie shrugged. "You doubt my father's word? He's a gentleman."

"But he's a fisherman," said Jenny, with a dazzling smile.

Fishing Grandpop Style

Rowing a boat out from shore, Grandpop looks for a likely spot, perhaps near some lily pads for pumpkinseed. These small fish are made of sterner stuff than sunfishes. When one hits, there's no nibble; just an explosion of thrashing and jumping, and a tussle before the flopping little fish is brought to the boat. A great deal of napping can occur on these trips.

But there is more. A good-sized crappie, perhaps two or three pounds, might be mooching around in deeper water, near a sunken tree or submerged rock. He'll run with the bait, too, and put a bend in the rod as he carries out line against the fast-clicking drag mechanism of the reel.

In a clear channel, from the bank nearby or from a boat anchored above the chosen spot, Grandpop can angle for catfish cruising the bottom. The bait can be practically anything; catfish aren't choosy. But when a catfish strikes, perhaps after nosing around the worm, pork-rind, or chunk of bait-fish, there will be a tussle.

Old Man in Fishing Boat (1930) 39

Further out, taking turns with friends at the oars, the angler can give trolling a whirl, using a plug to attract a white perch—a jumper that is just as fond of little live minnows in calm water as he is by the wooden facsimile on the troll.

When the fisherman goes trolling, he takes a big step toward the more sophisticated forms of fishing. He realizes that if he casts his bait or lure, he can reach fish in hard-to-get-at places like rock-strewn shallows, patches of lily pads, or eddies or holes beyond his reach. He can also simulate trolling by casting far out and reeling the line toward him. He goes after the fish who forage among weeds and other aquatic growth, and he uses any of the plugs or lures designed to resist getting snagged or fouled in the underwater foliage. Using his casting skills, he competes on the surface with swarming flies and midges for the attention of the fish. Fishermen learn the techniques of twitching or jerking the line to simulate the motions of different insects. Casting requires not only additional skills, but more energy and movement. It is active sport.

Men Are Fish (1936)

Another Way

The great appeal of spinning gear is in its lightness. Since the line flies quickly and easily off the reel, the spin-fisherman can use a lighter line, a shorter, more flexible rod, and achieve longer casts with lighter lures. The mechanics of casting are simpler, and the fisherman can play and land both small fish and large ones with the same rig.

Spin-fishermen use two types of casts. In both the rod is held in a fairly relaxed grip (with the forefinger controlling the line) so the wrist is limber and free to provide the flex and power for the cast.

The fisherman begins the shorter cast with both his forearm and the rod horizontal. He uses his wrist to tilt the rod upward, keeping his arm horizontal. This causes a slight arc in the rod, and the weighted lure, hanging six inches from the tippet, swings outward. The angler keeps his forearm horizontal, and raises the rod-tip upward, to an angle of about 45 degrees. Now, with no movement by the hand, the weight of the lure causes it to swing further outward. At this point, using both hand and wrist, but still with the forearm horizontal, the angler flexes the rod backward, over his head. When the rod is at its extreme rear position and the lure has completed its rearward swing above the tip, the fisherman gently snaps the rod forward. The lure swings up and over the rod-tip. When the tip of the bowed rod reaches a forward angle of approximately 45 degrees and the lure is swinging above and ahead of it, the angler releases the line (by lifting his forefinger or pressing the release on a push-button reel). The line runs out straight from the rod-tip, and the lure drops into the water. Throughout, the fisherman's forearm has remained horizontal.

The Fisherman (1916) 43

The power cast, for longer distances or with especially light lures, involves the entire arm. It follows the same routine as the shorter cast, beginning with the forearm horizontal, rod held in a relaxed fashion. But the first flex of the rod is strengthened with a slight lift of the forearm, as is the overhead flexing, made more extreme with the arm and forearm, which also add authority to the forward snap. The result is a much longer cast.

The timing of the line release is crucial. The ideal is a flat, precise cast. If the release is too soon the lure sails up in the air, making it impossible to control the length or direction of the cast. Too late and the lure will plop in the water at the fisherman's feet.

Spin-casters place a lot of importance on rod action—the relative rigidity of the rod-tip. For open water and slow-flowing rivers and streams, they use a light rod, with reel and line to match. When they fish a swift-running stream, they use a somewhat heavier tip and stronger line. They use stiff-tipped rods and heavier lines in windy conditions to cast heavy spoons and plugs, to strike hard at larger fish, and to pull the fish through weeds and other underwater growths.

In retrieving the line, the rod is held just above the horizontal, especially with a surface lure, or with sinking lures in shallow water. An important function for all rods is to ease the pressure on the line. A run by a heavy fish that would snap the line if the rod were held straight out is reduced to a bowed rod if the tip is raised to a higher angle. This is what makes it possible for the angler to use lightweight tackle for large fish, and enjoy the heightened action. The even tension on the line from a steeper angle will also keep the line from snagging on brush or snags. Anglers snap the rod in various ways to make the lure move as natural bait would.

Except to give the fish line to run with, the angler strives to keep the rod at a right angle to the line. This cushions the line so that it will not break from the direct pressure of a large fish's struggles. With a large battler applying plenty of pull against both line and rod, the fisherman tightens the drag for better control.

Turn of the Tide (1937)

In the Deep

Even though casting is more difficult with the bait-casting rod and reel, the rig has many devotees among fresh-water fishermen and surf-casters. People who do not cast at all use the gear for its original, bait-fishing purpose. In addition, the bait-casting rod and reel, in very heavy versions, is standard for deep-sea fishing and trolling.

It is the rig for big fish like pike, muskellunge, and salmon, its partisans say. The reel is stronger, size for size, than spinning reels, and the drag is better. So the bait-caster loads on heavy live baits and goes after the big ones.

Sport (1939)

Showing the Catch for the Day (1961)

The bait-caster has more things to do and more things to worry about than the spin-caster. He uses the same motions in casting, but relies on a longer rod and a more strenuous effort to overcome the friction on the line as it rolls off the spool. The spin-fisherman holds the rod with his right hand throughout, and turns the reel-handle with his left. The bait-caster must switch the rod from right hand to left after the cast, so he can operate the reel handle with his right hand.

But the great difference is the importance of keeping control of the line. During the windup for the cast, the bait-caster keeps his thumb on the spool, releasing it to begin the cast. But he must keep that thumb hovering over the spool, and put the brakes on the line quickly when the lure reaches its destination. If he fails in this, even slightly, the penalty is disaster. When the pressure exerted by the weight at the far end of the line ceases, the spool keeps spinning out line. The result is a backlash, and the fisherman faces a half-hour or more of hard and exasperating work to untangle the snarled line. The spin-fisherman, whose spool does not revolve, has no such problem.

Having avoided the backlash and landed his bait or lure in the spot he wanted, the bait-fisherman switches hands. He holds the rod in his left hand now, forward of the reel, and grasps the line (always atop the rod with bait tackle) between thumb and forefinger. This places a slight tension on the line as the right hand reels it in. At the same time, the left hand manipulates the angle of the rod and the motion of the lure.

Control of line tension with the thumb is important throughout casting, playing, and landing. With big fish and hard runners, the drag mechanism takes over to maintain steady pressure. The tried and true fisherman has a similar creed to that of the United States Post Office "Neither rain nor . . . ."

Norman Rockwell Visits a Family Doctor (1947)

On the Fly

Trout and salmon fishermen are the prime practitioners of the art of fly-fishing. Associations of trout and salmon fly-fishermen were among the first advocates of conservation practices to preserve both the wilderness environment and to halt and reverse the pollution of rivers and streams. For many years, as individuals and through their organizations, trout fisherman have doubled as missionaries, urging their fellow fishermen to release catches so they can reproduce and increase the falling fish population.

Their approach to fishing is in keeping with this genteel frame of mind. While bass fishermen may refer to their quarry as "hawgs," trout devotees use such nicknames as "brownies" and "dollies," and angle for them in an artistic and pleasurable way, usually in idyllic wilderness settings.

"Trouble with you trout fishermen," said Cousin Calvin, "is you're elitists and snobs."

Along the Trout Stream (1916)

Charlie and John took this tolerantly. "You're thinking of dry-fly fishermen like Dad," Charlie said. "Us wet-fly folks are common as dirt. Even Dad's been known to put on a worm now and then."

"It's not just that," Cousin Calvin continued as John refreshed his drink. "Thank you very much. You're behind the times. You go fishing in your tweeds, on those exclusive little trout streams, with your waders and vests and funny hats, and you use those old split bamboo rods and reels that won't reel in line. You haven't changed a thing in hundreds of years. You're sticks in the mud."

"That's the fun," John said. "The fish haven't changed. Why should we? It's sport."

"What about progress?" Cousin Calvin asked. "We have fun, too, and you know an eight-pound largemouth will leap and jump and try to pull you out of the boat if he can. Now that's sport. But we're scientific about it, that's all."

"Boy, you sure are," said Charlie. "And you people really look efficient in those jump suits with patches all over them. I've been out for bass with my son, Cliff, and his wife, Alice, down in Louisiana. Good lord! Great big 85 horsepower fiberglass boats. They used to use those five horsepower wooden john boats, remember? And all those plugs and jigs and spinners. If the noise from those boats doesn't daze those bass, the electronic gadgets will. Those little depth-finders to locate the deep holes, complete with computer read-outs. I'm surprised the bass don't just give up and jump in the boat when they see you coming."

Along the Trout Stream (1920)

"You forgot the radar sets," laughed Cousin Calvin. "You can see single fish or schools of them, and you can tell what kind of fish they are. And you sure get a lot of fish on a good day."

"So do we," said John, "the old-fashioned way."

"Ah well," said Cousin Calvin, "It's all fishing, isn't it?"

Fly-fishing demands physical effort, and precise coordination of rod, reel, and line. The trout or salmon angler is busy when he's fishing.

The demands begin with the cast, in which the fly-fisherman relies to a greater extent than others on his rod. The flies are negligible as weights, and while the line is heavy at the forward end, it is not heavy enough to pull line off the reel. To overcome these factors, the fly-fisherman uses a longer rod than any other, and varies the flexibility of the rod-tip to meet the needs of the moment. A rigid tip action will whip the line out a fair distance. A less rigid tip is used for a shorter cast with a dry fly, and with wet flies. For even shorter casts, with both wet and dry flies or light baits, a rod with a limber tip is used.

Making Good in a Boys' Camp (1917)

In addition, the fly-fisherman relies on a wide repertoire of casts. They have in common the quality of grace. As the caster swings and vibrates the rod to charge it with energy for the throw, the line whirls and billows, forming fanciful patterns in the air.

With the fish hooked, the fisherman maintains pressure by raising and lowering the rod-tip, at the same time looping in line with his other hand. He gives the fish line by paying out the line in hand, and also retrieves it by hand.

Trout fishing differs from other forms of angling in that both the equipment and the attitude of the fisherman dictate that the fish is never pulled in by the obviously greater strength of the fisherman. The fish is ready for landing only when it is exhausted by the struggle. The angler holds the rod high, gathering all slack line. If possible, the fish is upstream and drifts back and into the net. If the fisherman is going to release the fish, he holds him carefully in the water until he is sure he has recovered from the shock and exhaustion of the battle, and able to function fully. Then he lets him go and makes his next cast.

Retirement (1963)

Go Home (1918)

Chapter 4
Tackle and Gear

The Lone Fisherman

Many a fish is still caught on a crudely baited hook tied directly to a hand-line, and the fish is not always humble. Using a worm on a hook, attached to some line, with the bait in a tin can, many a boy would stand under a large, shady elm on the bank of a pond. Casting underhand into the current, he would pull out trout in great numbers.

His father and almost all other sport fishermen used rods and reels and artificial lures. Their ideal is to use a rod and line whose strength will be tested to the breaking point by the fish the angler expects to hook. Avoiding the break and landing the fish, in turn, are the tests of these fishermen's skill. But the boy felt as many thrills with his gear.

About Lines

Modern lines are made of synthetics, and the general rule is to use as light a line as practical. In spin-casting, bait-casting, and trolling, the bait or lure provides the weight needed to carry to the required distance. In non-casting forms of fishing, weights are attached to resist movement by winds and current. In fly-fishing, since the lure and hook are of no significant weight, the line itself provides the weight for the cast. So it tapered, thicker and heavier at the business end.

Boys Fishing (1961)

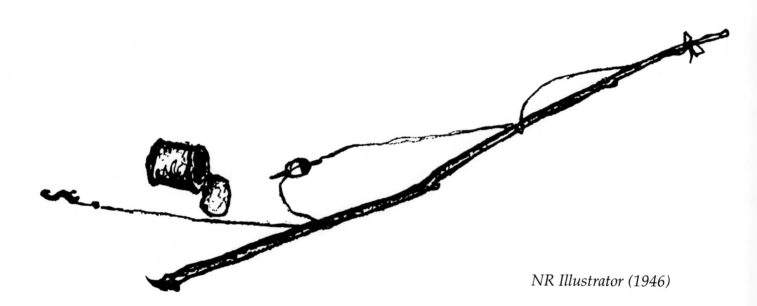

NR Illustrator (1946)

Rods

Traditionally, fishing rods were made of cane and split bamboo, as well as harder, less flexible woods for the deep-sea fisherman. Much craftsmanship went into the old rods, and many are still in use, much favored and coddled by their owners, who swear by their balance, flexibility, and grace. For people who can afford it, such rods are still made and painstakingly repaired and restored by craftsmen of the old school. Nevertheless, the fiber-glass rods manufactured today—as well as those made to order and carefully balanced and adjusted by modern craftsmen—also give their owners pleasure, and do the job. Except for offsetting to bring the reel closer to the thumb of the hand holding the rod, the modern rod looks and functions much as rods always have. The modern fisherman, however, tends to use a shorter, lighter rod, to match the lighter gear that he feels makes for better sport.

Whatever the material, rods are made in a single section or in two or three pieces, joined for action by metal ferrules at the joints. Two- and three-piece rods are less awkward for travel, but the ferrule joint inhibits flexibility. Also, they require great care in jointing and unjointing. The angler must line up the line guides precisely before finally pushing the ferrule into the socket, to avoid harming the joint by twisting the pieces afterward to align them. It is standard practice to lubricate the ferrule lightly by rubbing it against the angler's nose. It will then be easier to separate the pieces.

Bait-casting Rods

Bait-casting rods, too, are offset these days to give better access to the reel. Other than that, and the new materials, they have not changed in hundreds of years. The reel is affixed on top of the rod, and the line guides, on top of the rod, are smaller than those of the spinning rod.

Spinning Rod

The spinning reel requires a different sort of rod from the bait-casting or fly-casting rod. The line guides, through which the line passes from the reel to the tip, are larger toward the reel, since they must not hamper the coils of line traveling so rapidly out of the reel in a cast. It also has a weighted tip, to increase the flexing for a cast. When a closed-face spinning reel is used, it hangs down from the handle, which is often offset to accommodate it. A light to ultra-light rod, five to six feet long, is best for small trout and panfish; a light to medium rod, up to 6.5 feet, for larger fish; and a medium to heavy rod, as long as 7.5 feet, for big bass, pike, and other heavyweights, or in difficult conditions.

Spinning Reels

Certainly there have been many innovations in fishing tackle. One is the spinning reel, devised in England and enthusiastically adopted in this country. This new departure turned the spool 180 degrees, to the same axis as the rod. This way, the line loops or spins out from the spool, instead of unwinding from it. The spinning reel revolutionized casting. It cuts down on friction to permit longer casts and lighter lures, and virtually eliminates backlashes. A more recent innovation in the spinning reel is the push-button reel, which has a lever to release line otherwise held back by the fisherman's thumb.

Fly-fishing Reels

For fly-fishing, the chief use of the reel is to store line. The line is almost always looped out by hand for the cast. The reel is only used to play such large fish as salmons and steelheads, and it makes only one revolution for each turn of the handle. Fly-fishing reels are quite large, both to balance the rod and to carry a great length of braided "running" line, tied to the tapered line that is cast. However, there is an automatic reel that will now retrieve line and avoid the time-consuming business of stripping it in by hand to prepare for a new cast. Some reels have built-in drag adjustments, mainly to keep the line from going out too fast, but also handy for playing large fish.

Bait-casting Reels

With the bait-casting reel, used for every sort of fishing but fly-casting, the line unwinds as the spool revolves. The reel originated in Europe, in the Eighteenth Century, and the originals imported into this country made one revolution for each turn of the handle. It was George Snyder, of Paris, Kentucky, who applied Yankee ingenuity to the reel. In 1810, he invented the modern "multiplying" reel, geared so that the spool makes four revolutions to a turn of the handle. Another modern improvement, also standard in spinning reels, is drag control. This prevents the spool from running freely. The drag mechanism can be adjusted to function as a heavy brake or a light restraint, as required. It prevents a big fish from running freely with the line, and is useful in trolling from a moving boat.

Three Boys Fishing (1937)

The Fly-rod

This rod has changed very little through the years, and it differs significantly from the spinning rod and the bait-casting rod. The reel is mounted to the rear of the handle, which is always of cork on a fly-rod. Also, on fly-rods, the reel hangs downward. The line guides are quite small, since the line is fed directly, although the first guide is usually round and a bit larger than the further ones.

Fly fishermen tend to be purists and to value flexibility, so the incidence of bamboo rods is probably greatest among them. Fly-rods run longer than the others, though light weight is valued.

The fisherman in Norman Rockwell's April Fools day picture pokes gentle fun at this venerable institution.

April Fool: Fishing (1945)

Mermaid (1955)

Chapter 5
Baits and Lures

The Amazing Bait

Most fish, including the much-esteemed trouts, are undiscriminating feeders. The varieties that most interest sport fisherman take enthusiastic interest in food. Some eat as much as a fifth of their own weight each day. Crawfish and other crustaceans, grubs, worms, insects and their larvae, other fish including small members of their own species are acceptable baits. The sportier breeds appear curious and venturesome at times. Salmons, shads, and trout varieties that migrate from the sea to their native fresh-waters do not, on the highest authority, feed on their spawning runs. But apparently they like an occasional snack on the road. They provide sport for anglers by snapping in passing at the artificial flies offered them. Pork rind—the gamier the better—is a great attraction to catfish and other varieties who couldn't possibly ever see it except on a hook, any more than the dough-balls they also relish, mixed up with cotton batting to keep them intact in the water. Big bass seem territorial and grumpy; they lunge at bright and shiny objects that invade their turf.

To a large extent, these feeding habits are the basis for sport fishing. The trick is to figure out where and when the fish are lurking or hunting, and to offer the bait or lure in a way that will seem natural. One wonders what bait this fisherman's catch required.

Natural Baits

Basic fishing is for panfish—the sunfish, bluegill, crappie, and yellow and white perch to be found in almost any American lake. These fish will rise to flies, but they are a good bet for the beginner on basic, natural baits. An earthworm is a surefire bait for the sunfish. The same worm will also attract larger yellow perch. White perch, who travel nearer the surface, go for live minnows. Minnows are a separate species that includes some large fish, but fishermen use the term to cover any small bait-fish. Bluegills, of the same family as sunfish, will take worms, grubs, and minnows. So will larger fish like bass and pickerels, but for them, results are better with small sunfishes and perches on the hook, or with shiners, dace, chubs, darters, sticklebacks, crawfish, grasshoppers, and frogs.

In recent years technology has solved the problem of deterioration and waterlogging in such baits as worms and eels and pork rind. Lifelike plastic and rubber replicas are now used to successfully simulate them, and frogs, bugs, and other tidbits.

Boy with Fishing Pole (1919)

Spinners and Spoons

Fishermen believe the original spoon was the result of a lakeful of perverse fish refusing to nibble at anything an angler dangled before them. A frustrated fisherman cut the handle off a spoon, attached the spoon to a leader and a hook to the spoon-bowl. He cast it. It wobbled and flashed in the water as he reeled it back in, and time after time, fish struck on it. With more sophisticated hardware, this has been going on ever since. Spoons come in all shapes, sizes and colors now, but they all wobble and flash like the original, in a way that seems to fascinate any fish of spirit.

The spinner is an extension of the same idea (a spin-off, perhaps). It is mounted on a shaft that revolves in the water rather than wobbling, and it attracts the fish's attention in the same gratifying way as its precursor.

Men Are Fish (1936)   77

Plugs

The first plugs were carved fish-like shapes, perhaps from bungs or plugs for barrels, later from broom handles, with fish-hooks attached. They were cast with bait-casting rods and retrieved by reeling in line. Often enough to encourage plug-carving, a hungry fish would strike at the fish-like carving during the retrieval. Latter-day plugs, still carved from wood, are refined and balanced in ways that yield a wide variety of gyrations and jumps during the retrieve—all things to all fishes. The shapes now resemble frogs and mice as well as bait-fish, and they are painted in bright but realistic colors. Spinners, fins, and fluttery skirts and feathers are often attached, to increase curiosity and drawing power.

Man Fishing (1926)

Bass Bugs

Bass bugs are a specialist plug, an intermediate link between the plugs and the artificial fly. Bass plugs are carved of wood and painted, but too large for most trouts or panfish. They are designed for bass and for larger trout, both of which feed on insects and small creatures they encounter in the water. There are many patterns, and the carved wood is supplemented with hairs, simulated wings, and streamers. A few examples are a wooden bug, trimmed with hair; an entire bug made of deer-hair, with long wings made of fiber; a wooden plug with hair and feather streamers; and one of long deer-hairs tied to resemble frogs or mice. Bass bugs are made to float on the surface. The angler simulates the motions he thinks will attract the fish by manipulating the line and jerking the rod-tip.

Barefoot Boy Dreaming (1922)

Artificial Flies

Many fish, including humble and relatively sluggish ones, will take artificial flies, but the original quarry it was meant to attract were trouts and salmons, whose diet includes larvae in various stages of development, as well as flies and insects of all sorts.

The classic fly-fisherman Izaak Walton wrote in his angler's bible that the last trout he had landed was caught on a worm. Trout fishermen devised the artificial fly as the result of their ancient obsession with the quarry's feeding habits. They learned early that trout eat the larvae of various flies, as well as aquatic nymphs (advanced larvae, often snatched as they drift to the surface, where they will hatch), and newly hatched flies of all sorts that swarm on the surface of pools and streams. They soon discovered that if artificial flies could be tied that resembled the sub-surface larvae or the nymphs or flies, a fellow could catch more fish. Particularly if he could match the larvae that was popular in the spot he visited; especially if the flies matched in shape, color, and behavior the insects that were swarming that very day on the trout waters. The study goes on today. Fishermen have long studied the contents of fish they caught to discover what they had been feeding on.

Dry flies float or skitter on the surface to imitate the actions of emerging and adult insects. Wet flies are cast below the surface, to sink to the bottom or float midway, aping larvae sacs and insects in intermediate stages that rise to the surface to hatch. Flies are also tied to resemble ants, grasshoppers, and bugs and insects that do not exist, but might tickle a fish's appetite. The dreaming young man may just come up with a new fly, inspired by his visiting nymphs.

Summertime: Boy Fishing (1933) 83

Going and Coming (1947)

Chapter 6
The Fish

So Many Fish, So Little Time

There are about 4,000 varieties of fish in North American waters, and a lot more in the ocean areas where Americans pursue fish. Just about every fish has its devotees. The voracious catfish, sunfishes, bream, and the others lumped as panfish that are usually the juvenile fisherman's first catch; through the ranks to the bonefish and the oddly named and rarely captured permit of the Florida inlets; to the lordly salmons and trouts and the majestic marlins and sailfish. These species show varying degrees of elusiveness, of beauty, and fight. Every fisherman knows there is no fish more delicious than the one he just caught and cleaned.

The Trout

Most likely, the first sporting fish the Pilgrims encountered was the brook trout, native to the cold-water streams of the Northeast. It is called the squaretail in parts of New England, and the speckled trout in Canada. It is also called the "native trout," which it is. Both rainbows and brown trouts are imports, introduced into eastern streams in the late Nineteenth Century.

Sea trout, the sea-going variety of brook trout, is highly prized by surf-casters and ocean anglers for the two years it spends in salt water.

The sea trout has a dark back and silvery sides, marked with reddish spots. After a week or two back in fresh water, it recovers the original brook trout characteristics: a brownish sheen, a red horizontal stripe that also colors the pectoral fins, and large white-bordered spots above.

The size of brook trout varies in direct proportion to the size of the streams in which they live and feed. They reach two pounds or more, even ten pounds, in large streams, but in small, steep mountain brooks or pools, two pounds is a prodigious catch.

The brown trout (salmo trutta) is a true trout, the only trout native to the British Isles and Europe. It first immigrated to North America in 1883, in the form of 80,000 eggs on a German liner, consigned to the New York State hatchery at Cold Spring Harbor.

The importation was needed because of the decline in size and numbers of the brook trout. Its range was small then, limited to the cool streams of the Northeast, the section of the country that first experienced dense population, industrialization, deforestation, and water pollution.

The brown was not immediately popular, and was considered a coarse inferior to the brookie, both as a fighter and table delicacy. It was soon evident that the brown would quickly devour the smaller brook trout in any stream it entered. But the brown trout had the great compensating virtue that it tolerates both warmer water and a greater degree of impurity than the brook trout. Also, anglers found, the brown grew to a larger size, it took flies readily, and fought with spirit. It even made heart-stopping leaps out of the water in its efforts to shake off the barb. Brook trout fight well, but they don't go in for aerial acrobatics.

It is a pretty fish as well, with many color variations that depend on its locale. Reaching maturity in a cold stream, it is olive brown or green at the back, graduating to lighter shades on its sides and a bright golden yellow on the belly. Black or dark brown spots fleck the upper sides. Below the dorsal fin, the brown is sprinkled with red spots, sometimes encircled by blue rings. The fins are yellow-green, sometimes with brown or red spots. Unfortunately for the color scheme, the usual brown reaches maturity in a hatchery, and is apt to be handsome but less colorful.

There is a seagoing variety of brown trout, both in New England and Canada. Like the sea-run brown of Europe, this fish is often confused with the Atlantic salmon in its salt-water sojourn. European fishermen call it a salmon trout.

Interestingly enough, many male trouts (including the brown) will fertilize the eggs of the female salmon in its upcountry fresh water spawning grounds, if no male salmon is around.

Rainbow Trout

The rainbow trout is the spectacular western cousin of the elegant brook and the hardy brown. It is larger than the brown and has the reputation of giving the hardest fight.

The rainbow takes on the names of the Western localities where it is found: Shasta, Klamath River, McCloud River, and others. A close Canadian cousin, the Klamloops trout, has been colonized throughout the Western states and Canadian provinces.

In all its varieties, the rainbow is a startlingly beautiful fish. It sports no spectrum of colors, though, but a pink-to-lavender lateral stripe from eye to tail. The upper sides and back are green-bronze, dappled with small dark spots that extend to the stripe but not to the silvery belly. It grows darker as its spawning time nears, and the stripe turns scarlet.

When the rainbow takes a lure, it puts up a spectacular fight, unique among even the gamest trouts. It leaps into the air in its attempts to shake off the hook, and leaps again and again. Often it appears to dance on its tail.

Like the East Coast trouts, the rainbow has a family branch that periodically takes to the sea. The steelhead is the seagoing rainbow. It develops a silvery color and loses its stripe at sea, but quickly recovers them when it returns to fresh water.

The rainbow is, in fact, a hardy and tenacious fish. In its Western habitat it faces the same predators as its Eastern cousins: fishermen, pollution, mink, otter, watersnakes, snapping turtles, bass and pickerel, larger trouts, and kingfishers, ospreys, eagles, and other birds of prey. It also has to contend with bears in the northern reaches of its territory, as well as dams. Yet it multiplies.

Schoolboy Gazing Out Window (1922)

89

Sunapee Trout

The Sunapee trout is a small species, native to Sunapee Lake, New Hampshire, and other small, deep lakes in Maine, New Hampshire, and Vermont.

The Sunapee likes deep, chill water. Its back and upper sides are olive- to sea-green, and the lower flanks are orange (to account for the name "golden trout" often applied to it). This orange turns to a bright red in breeding males. The belly has been described as "brilliant red," as well as "conspicuously white," to justify another appellation, "white trout." Its spots are either whitish, pale yellow, orange, or pinkish, and its tail is forked.

Blueback Trout

The blueback is a State-of-Maine native, restricted even in its days of abundance to that state's Rangeley Lakes. It is a slim and small fish, rarely exceeding a pound, and a retiring one. It prefers deep, cold water, and seldom feeds on the surface, so it is no target for the fly-fisherman.

But it is a beauty. Its back is steel-blue and iridescent (brownish in some cases), turning lighter blue and then silver down the sides. The belly is a pale yellowish pink or salmon-colored. The bellies of males about to breed turn deep red, as do the lower fins, which at other times are orange or pink. Spots, when they occur, are whitish or creamy, and numerous. The top of the head, as well as the snout, is often a metallic blue-black.

Lake Trout

The lake trout requires deep water—at least 50 feet, and the deeper the better. It spends the summer in the cooler water of the depths, and must be fished there, as deep as 300 feet, with a stout rod and heavy lures or bait. But the laker takes to the shallows in spring and fall. In those waters, it will take flies readily, as well as lures on trolls.

It is a formidable fish, second in size only to the chinook salmon and dwarfing the other trouts.

In smaller lakes, less abundant in the alewives, whitefish, ciscoes, and smelts on which the lake trout forage, the catches are more modest, but fish of 15 to 25 pounds are fairly normal.

In its wide range, the lake trout takes on a variety of colorations, but its distinctive characteristics include its deeply forked tail and many spots that range from off-white to pale yellow (reddish in Alaska). The background color varies: gray, deep brown, or green-blue on the back, fading to a lighter and iridescent blue on the sides and to a white or delicate pink belly.

Golden Trout

The golden trout is a jewel, even among the handsome trout family. It requires clear, cold waters and an altitude of 8,000 feet or more to thrive. Those special conditions exist in a small area in California, in the lakes and streams of the Sierra crest, along the Kern River watershed, north to El Dorado County.

The golden trout has a gray-green back, and its upper sides are olive-yellow, with sparse dark spots. A broad lateral band of deep pink or red, overlaid with blue-black parrs (smudge-like marks, similar to those that mark the young salmons called parrs), sometimes spotted, runs along the sides. Below that band, the fish is of a golden yellow color that may extend to the belly, or may turn to orange or pink as it descends.

The golden is a game fish, though not an epic battler like the rainbow. It does not reach great size. There is no seagoing variety, since the golden could not survive the low altitudes and warm waters involved in a migration to the ocean. Usually, it spawns in its native stream and eventually migrates between that stream and a lake in the same restricted range. Some goldens, isolated in mountain ponds and lakes, manage to spawn in those waters, and grow to greater size than those in streams.

Cutthroat Trout

The cutthroat gets its name not from its disposition but from the slash of red below its jaw. The cutthroat strains have interbred for a long time, and they take different appearances in various parts of their range, apart from the red streak that accounts for the name. Generally, the back and upper sides are of a grayish green color, interrupted by a pink-tinted lateral streak on the sides. The belly is white, and the fish often have dark spots that extend to the fins, which in the cutthroat have a pink tinge. But a cutthroat may have golden spots mixed with the dark ones, or even a stripe like the rainbow's.

The cutthroat is full of fight. It may, like the rainbow, leap spectacularly and thrash on the surface. Or it may stay below, like a brook trout, and go as deep as it can.

The cutthroat reaches great size. Cutthroats in streams and rivers run smaller than those in lakes.

Dolly Varden

The Dolly Varden trout is a pretty fish with a bad reputation. Commercial salmon fishermen in Alaska claim it feeds in great schools on freshly spawned sockeye salmon eggs, as well as preying on young salmon as they head downstream for their sojourn in the Pacific.

There are variations in the Dolly Varden's colors. Usually the back is dark green, deep brown, or even black. The upper sides are bronze and iridescent down to the lateral, gray-green below that. The belly is white. The fish is dappled with pale or white spots above the lateral that give way to red or orange tints on the lower sides. Ventral and anal fins range from pink to carmine, like the brook trout. The other fins often have a reddish edge.

The Salmon

The fame of the Atlantic salmon is understandable. It achieves tremendous speeds to launch its prodigious leaps to scale rapids and falls and uses tail and fins in the struggle upstream to spawn in its home waters. This great fish puts up a heroic struggle against the hook, and challenges the angler with its sheer strength and spirit. Its fight is similar to that of the brook trout and brown trout, but the struggle is on a grander scale.

It is during their time at sea that the salmon gain their size. The older and larger salmon are at their peak when they begin the spawning voyage—strong, muscular, bulging with the fat on which they will subsist for the long trek. They are bronzed in the upper body, silvery below, with a sprinkling of dark spots on the head and the gill covers, as well as a few cross-hatches on the back and upper sides.

As they proceed, they grow thinner and almost waste away before they reach home waters. They are buffeted by rapids, bashed against rocks, preyed upon by bears and other predators, including birds of prey. They lose their silvery sheen on the way, and turn a dull red, with large black spots. The males become mottled and blotched, covered with a slimy coating and afflicted by a spreading fungus. Many die of exhaustion or wounds. The survivors of the ordeal and the spawning are in even worse condition for the trip back to sea. They are accurately dubbed "spent salmon," and "black salmon," as well as "slinks," and "kelts." At this stage, they are ugly, weak, unfit to eat. They recover at sea, and return to spawn again two or three times during their life spans.

Salmon are not supposed to feed on their upstream run, but the big, silvery fish will take both wet and dry flies. The resemblance to trout-fishing ends there. The salmon need not be cautiously stalked, like the trout, and it will run immediately, and fast, when it strikes. Trying to hook a salmon is the best way to lose it. But once the salmon hooks himself, he requires much more line than a trout. The fisherman releases line when the salmon runs, and takes it back when the pressure is off. Finally, after a spectacular series of rolls, jumps, runs, and twists, the fisherman lands his fish.

In the Land of Gold (1915)

Landlocked Salmon

Landlocked salmon mimic the seagoing variety. They are born in tributary streams and after two or three years they migrate to the lakes, where they grow fairly rapidly on a diet of smaller fish and insects. Females of four to five years old and males of three to four make the spawning run to the native grounds, in mid-October in the northernmost lakes and late November in Lake George, New York, the present southern extreme of the landlockeds.

The best fishing for landlockeds is in the Maine lakes in early spring, when the ice first breaks up. Then the smelt, a staple of the landlocked diet, are beginning their spawning run, and the salmon attack them, together with anything else that seems interesting. In the summer heat, they retreat to deep water but rise occasionally to take flies or lures on trolls. Each fall, when the landlockeds are feeding at the mouths of streams to fatten up for their own spawning run, the fishing is good for fly-fishermen and for those who troll with feathered streamers.

The landlocked salmon is much larger than the trout on which it also feeds, but is smaller than the seagoing Atlantic salmon. The fish is just as game, pound for pound, as the sea-run variety; a great leaper and a determined fighter.

The Stay at Homes (1927)

Across the Threshold (1914)

Chinook Salmon

The chinook salmon was named after the local Chinook Indians, who lived in comparative luxury on abundant harvests of salmon—so much so that they formally celebrated the spring and fall runs of the fish. The Indians reaped the plentiful fish with hooks, traps, seines, gill nets, harpoons, dip nets, and even shot them with bows and arrows. They feasted on the catch, and smoked the excess salmon, dried it, and traded what they didn't need with other tribes.

The chinook is the largest of all salmons, running as high as 100 pounds and averaging 25. It shows a penchant for big rivers, like the Yukon and Columbia, and it travels great distances in its upstream migrations. When the young hatch, they tend to head for sea almost immediately from southern rivers, although some 20 percent remain in the river for a year. In the northernmost rivers, most young chinooks stay a full year, feeding chiefly on plankton, insects and larvae, and tiny fish, before migrating in schools, as three-inch parrs.

At sea, the chinooks thrive on a diet dominated in the first year by the "red feed" that is responsible for the red color of their flesh, the euphausiid shrimp. In four or five years, full grown and fattened for the coming ordeal, the adult chinooks head home to spawn.

At this point, the chinook is at its most handsome. Its back and upper sides are of deep greenish blue, lightening toward the lateral line to a bright silver that extends to the gill covers and cheeks. The dorsal fin is dark, the lower fins pale. Black spots speckle the upper sides. Even before they enter the river, some of the fish become reddish in the belly and lower fins. Once in fresh water, the chinook grows darker. By the time they reach their goal, the males are a muddy red, the females less so, and the males have developed a hooked jaw for use in spawning fights.

The chinook is highly rated as a gamefish. It strikes hard and runs hard, leaps high, and fights a stubborn fight. Anglers catch it much more often in the sea and in inlets at the mouths of rivers and streams, rather than on the spawning run. It shows little interest in artificial flies, but will hit spoons, spinners, and similar lures.

Pacific Salmon

There are five varieties of Pacific salmon, quite a distinct species from the Atlantic salmon. It is much more numerous than the Atlantic salmon, even though intense harvesting and pollution have reduced its population, and it is fished commercially in much greater volume. A distinctive characteristic of the Pacific salmon is that it makes only one return to its home in fresh water. There it spawns, and dies.

It has a vast range, from southern California to the Bering Strait in North America, and in Asia from Kamchatka south to Korea and Japan, as far east as the Aleutians and as far west as the Kuriles. Over the years, there have been numerous attempts to transplant both the Pacific and Atlantic salmon to each other's home waters, but no significant success has been achieved.

The Cruise of the Pegasus (1913)

Coho salmon

The coho, also called the silver salmon, has a smaller range than the chinook, from middle California to Alaska. It is a smaller fish, averaging five to twelve pounds in its southern range and slightly higher at the northern extreme. It spawns in small creeks as well as large rivers, and does not travel the great distances of the chinook. While the chinook make spawning runs both in spring and autumn, the coho returns to its home waters beginning in September. The spawning may be as late as November, or even January. The preliminaries are violent, with the males employing their exaggerated hook-jaws in the fights.

After hatching, the fry usually spend at least a year in fresh water. They move toward the ocean in small schools. At the time of its spawning run, the coho very much resembles the chinook. It is smaller and it has fewer spots with none on the dorsal fin or lower caudal. Its lower sides are even more brilliantly silver than the chinook's. It also loses its brilliant colors in fresh water, and turns a dull red. However, most observers agree that it retains its ocean tone longer, as well as its vigor.

Of the Pacific salmons, the coho is most frequently caught in freshwater streams, and the most likely bet for the fly-fisherman. Its fight more than matches that of the chinook, pound for pound. If anything, its champions say, the coho is the more ferocious fish, striking more readily and prolonging the struggle to test the angler.

Man Reading Vacation Pamphlet (1939)

Sockeye, Pink, and Chum Salmon

Unlike the chinook and coho, these varieties eat no fish while at sea, and are unlikely to take baits. They take artificial flies in their freshwater phases, and spoons and spinners both in salt and fresh water, and they give anglers a brisk fight.

The sockeye is the most valued commercial salmon. Its meat is of the deepest red known. In its ocean phase, it has a steel to grayish back and upper sides, turning deeper blue at the top of the head and upper gill covers. Its sides and belly are stark white, and it has few spots. As it nears spawning water, it turns muddy to bright red on the back and sides, and the bellies turn gray or mottled. After three to five years at sea, the sockeye travels hundreds of miles to spawn in the outlet or tributaries of its chosen lake.

The pink salmon is also called the humpback because of the bony hump in the back developed by the male at spawning time. It is the smallest of the Pacific salmons, seldom larger than seven pounds, but the most plentiful—a significant part of the commercial catch. It has a dark-brown to greenish blue back, liberally sprinkled with dark oval spots, and silvery sides and belly. It travels only a few miles upstream to spawn, and the young quickly migrate to sea, where they spend two years. It shows little or no interest in lures or baits.

Fishermen have no better luck with the chum salmon, also called dog salmon for its oversize head, exaggerated jaws, and its large canine teeth. The jaws extend and become hooked, and the teeth are even more pronounced at spawning time.

Despite this, the chum is a beauty. After three to six years at sea, when it prepares for its spawning run, it has a blue-gray back, often with a purple sheen, and silver sides. It averages eight to fifteen pounds. It is rarely tempted by lures or bait, but like all salmon, it is a fighter.

The Boys Aboard the 'Vanguard' (1914)

Grayling and Whitefish

The whitefish family of fish and its close cousins, the graylings, are related to the salmons and trouts. They are important food fishes, found mostly in northern waters, and mainly in lakes.

The arctic grayling, also called in various places the Rocky Mountain whitefish, Colorado grayling, Yellowstone grayling, Manistee herring, and even poisson bleu, still abounds in Canada and Alaska.

Depleted stocks of grayling are still found in the upper Missouri River in Montana, where Lewis and Clark mistook it for a trout, as well as the Madison and Jefferson rivers.

Usually, the grayling has a dark blue back and sides of purple-gray that are iridescent. It has 12 to 18 black spots on the forward sides. The head is small and is blue-bronze, with a bright blue mark on each lower jaw. The prominent dorsal fin is grayish, occasionally pale pink at its upper edge, and dotted with blue spots outlined with red. The male's dorsal fin is larger than the female's. The fish averages less than a pound in its American lairs, but two-pounders are not unusual further north.

The grayling is a fighter, like its trout cousins, and can be fished the same way. It may leap from the water to snap at a morsel, or sniff around it, just under the surface. It makes spectacular leaps.

Two Old Men and Dog: The Catch (1950)

Tides of Memory (1936)

Whitefish

Whitefishes differ from trout in their habit of traveling in schools, and none of the varieties is seagoing. They are native to the same lakes and streams as the Atlantic and Pacific salmons, as well as to many deep inland lakes in the Great Lakes region. They are an excellent food fish, both for men and for the lake trout, for whom ciscoes and chubs are a staple. They were once fished in great numbers commercially, chiefly in the Great Lakes, but no longer. Overfishing and the depredations of the sea lamprey have thinned them out.

They prefer deep water, except when they spawn, and grow to an average of 3.5 pounds, although 20-pounders have been recorded in Lake Superior. All the whitefish have weak mouths, and when hooked they must be gently played.

Shads

The herring family includes fresh- and salt-water varieties, as well as those that, like the shad, migrate between the two.

The American shad is the largest fish in the herring family, and like the herrings that spend their lives in salt water, it is an important food fish. From Colonial times until the 1950's, it was a staple dish all along the Atlantic seaboard, caught fresh in its yearly runs upstream to spawn and eaten year-round in its salted form. Then overfishing, pollution, and dams cut its numbers drastically. Nowadays, it is a luxury item. As ever, shad roe is greatly prized as a delicacy.

When it enters fresh water, the shad has a deep blue to blue-green back and silver sides. It has large, dark spots just back of the gill covers, and several smaller spots behind those. It is a gleaming, bright fish, especially in the large numbers in which it travels, and a slim, streamlined one.

In the northern rivers, both parents return to sea after spawning, but from Florida to North Carolina, most of the parents die after that first spawning. In the following fall, the three- to-five-inch fingerling shads run the gauntlet of predators and pollution to migrate to sea. There they remain and grow for three to five years before returning to spawn in their native rivers.

As the shad nears extinction as a commercial fish on both coasts, it has become increasingly popular as a sporting fish, particularly on eastern rivers. Even though they do not feed on their spawning runs, they lunge like salmon for flies and lures. Once hooked, they fight hard.

Fishes Like Neckties (1934)

The Common Cold (1945)

114

Smelts

The American smelt is of Atlantic origin and is one of the most delicious of fish. From times immemorial, the silvery little fish in great schools have made the early spring migration to their spawning waters in creeks and rivers from New England to the Great Lakes. Depleted though they may be, the American smelts support a large commercial industry.

The smelt attracts many thousands of ice-fishermen in wintertime, who throng to the many lakes of Michigan and Ontario, as well as Lake Erie and such eastern waters as the Finger Lakes and Lake Champlain. The smelts take cut bait, minnows, and bright lures.

Eulachon Smelt

Of the six migratory smelts on the Pacific coast, only the eulachon smelt is significant as a food fish. Its range is from Oregon to Alaska, and it migrates up the Columbia river and several of its tributaries in Oregon and Washington. It is a delicious fish that is also called the Columbia River smelt and the hooligan and oolichon, as well as the candlefish. This last refers to its body oils, solid at ordinary temperatures. In times past, the Indians actually dried this fish, ran a wick through it, and used it as a candle.

Chain Pickerel

The chain pickerel is found from Eastern Canada down to Florida, east of the Alleghenies in the northern United States, and as far west as Texas and Louisiana, as well as in Arkansas and Tennessee. It is the largest of the pickerels, normally running three pounds, but occasionally up to five. It is called in various localities the eastern pike, green pike, grass pike and grass pickerel, pond pickerel, and jack.

The chain pickerel gets its name from the dark bronze-green chainlike horizontal bars connected at times by vertical stripes, along its sides. These are spaced so closely in some varieties that they look like spots. In others, they are far apart. The sides are white to creamy yellow. There is a dark vertical bar below the eyes and a lighter one forward of them. The upper fins are greenish, sometimes with small dark spots on the caudal, and the lower fins are pale.

It lives in shallow and weedy streams and ponds, in clear and quiet waters. Chain pickerels are born hungry, anglers say, and stay that way. So voracious is the fish that it has often attacked a smaller trout as it was being reeled in by an angler.

It strikes hard, on baits and lures of all sorts, and the fight is furious but usually short-lived. The chain pickerel is also fair game for ice-fishermen.

The redfin, which does not have red fins, ranges the same areas as the chain pickerel, where it is variously called the banded, barred, brook, and little pickerel. The grass pickerel (little pickerel, grass pike) occurs from Iowa and Missouri to Wisconsin, Michigan, as well as in the Middle West and Canada. Both have backs of dark olive to bright green, sometimes bluish. The color lightens down the sides, which have rows of dark bars, and both have black bars below the eyes. The fish are avid feeders, but considered panfish rather than gamefish because of their small size.

Man Weighing Brook Trout (1939)

Northern Pike

This is a fabled fish in the north, with more than 40 local names, among which are American pike, great northern pike, Great Lakes pike, and jackfish. Like its cousins, it strikes hard at anything it sees. It is usually a solitary fish, intent and patient as it waits in the weeds for a passing mouthful. The pike starts off on minute aquatic life, but graduates to a catholic variety—all sorts of insects and crustaceans, minnows, perch, bluegills, suckers, trout, smaller pikes and muskies, worms, frogs, mice, snakes, and ducklings. It is estimated that a mature pike eats a fifth of its own weight, mostly in fish, every day.

The northern is a lean, long fish, green to olive on its back, fading to white or yellow in the belly. Lake Michigan pike have a reddish tinge.

Muskellunge

The average musky weighs 6 to 15 pounds, but many of 20 to 30 pounds are taken. Several of 60 pounds or more have been landed.

This greater size, added to the family's fighting disposition, make the musky a favored sporting fish throughout its range. It is a North American native, found from the St. Lawrence drainages in New York and Quebec to the Mississippi Valley. Muskies abound in Wisconsin and Minnesota. It takes several other names, including lunge, longe, tiger musky, and great pike.

It, too, is a solitary marauder, found in clear and shallow areas of larger lakes and slow-flowing rivers, but also in fairly weedless waters.

Pickerels, Northern Pike and Muskellunge

The pike family has five species in North America: three pickerels, one pike, and one muskellunge (musky). All are native to the continent except the pike, which also ranges over northern Europe and Asia.

It is probably the most voracious and savage family in fresh water. Its members lurk among the weeds in clear water, and strike hard and fast at anything that moves. The dash is swift, facilitated by a long, slender body, and the victim has little chance against the large, powerful jaws and strong teeth of these fish.

The five species range in size from the grass pickerel, barely a foot long at its largest, to five-foot muskellunges that weigh 60 pounds and more. Their prey ranges from minnows and crustaceans to large fish, waterfowl, snakes, and muskrats.

Apart from size, they look very much alike. The pickerels, however, have scales on the whole of the gill covers and cheeks; the northern pike has scales on the upper gill covers and the entire cheek; the muskellunge has scales only on the upper halves of the gill covers and cheeks.

The Gathering

So ends this chronicle of fishing with the family gathering on Memorial Day weekend, a custom begun by John at the summer place in the mountains. The family was growing larger every year. This Memorial Day, there was Kathleen, who had survived John, Charles and Jenny and their son and two daughters, and Cliff and Annie and their brood.

It all made a big racket, Charles thought, as he heaved himself down from the hammock between the cedars in the front yard. That was why he had passed up the afternoon's excursion of swimming and fishing at the far end of the lake. He stretched and decided on a walk. After a little more quiet and isolation, he might join Jenny and Kathleen, who were reading and knitting on the back porch.

He walked down to the lakeside, savoring the silence and the clean air. Sitting on the pier and kicking his legs over the water was his youngest grandson, John. He smiled as he tousled the boy's hair. His dad, when the boy was named, had thanked Charlie and Jenny for the honor but told them a little fellow like that could not be expected to carry a II attached to his name.

"What's up, Buster?" he asked. "No fishing or swimming?"

"I wanted to go, Grandpa, but I fell asleep in the apple tree and Mom told them to go off without me. And I wanted to learn about fishing. Daddy said he'd teach me, too."

So that was why he was moping. "Can't have that, Buster. But we can fish off this pier. Plenty of sunfish this end of the lake. Look," he pointed at the water under the boy's small feet. "See them nosing around down there? They're looking for things to eat."

"I see them! Wow! Let's catch 'em, Grandpa."

They hurried back to the house to get Charlie's lightest bait-rod. Back at the pier, the old man showed little John how to assemble the rod, attach the reel, bait the hook.

"I just dug these worms this morning," he said. "These will get us a fish, I think."

A few minutes later, John grew anxious.

"When are they going to bite?" he asked.

"Shh," said Charles. "You don't want to scare the fish. You've got to be patient, you know."

The nostalgia of this cherished sport not only remains fresh and clear in every fisherman's memories, but in the art of Norman Rockwell, as well.

Man and Boy Fishing (1929) 123

Picture Credits: